The Autist's cookbook,

recipes & tips for those in the autism spectrum

By

Viktor Schönberg

"The autist's cookbook, recipes and tips for those in the autism spectrum"

Second edition

Copyright © 2017 by Viktor Schönberg
All rights reserved. This book or any portion thereof
may not be reproduced or used in any manner whatsoever
without the express written permission of the publisher
except for the use of brief quotations in a book review.

About the author: Hello there, I'm Viktor. Thank you for opening and hopefully, reading this little book I've written. When I began writing this, I was doing it out of my own interest, as I had been collecting recipes for some time. Recipes, that are easy for me to read and cook. I myself have an Autism diagnosis as well as ADD, and I never really found a cookbook that were targeted for those with my condition and similar. Many of the recipes here can be altered to suit your preferred flavours, but the recipes are done after my taste. Some recipes are typical Swedish, but I have translated them as good as possible. I hope you'll enjoy this little book as much as I enjoyed writing it.

Viktor Schönberg

Table of Contents
1. Introduction
2. Bread & sandwich "cake"
3. Main courses
4. Desserts
5. Afterword

Introduction

Hello there, here I will write down some tips you can use as well as what tools I prefer to use while baking/cooking.

Tools

Let's face it, you can have the most exquisite ingredients, be a master chef. But if you don't have the right tools or don't take good care of your tools, cooking can be a nightmare and the results horrible.

I prefer to use wooden spoons when I'm cooking or baking, it might be just me, but I think it tastes better that way. Clean them by handwashing and dry them in cloth towels.

When frying fish or meat, I use metal tongs or spatula when flipping the meat. Those you can clean in the dishwasher.

Keep an array of knives, ranging from small to large ones, in your kitchen and sharpen them occasionally to keep them sharp.

Pans and pots

I'm raised with old style cooking, so using cast iron pots and pans is my preferable way. Of course, it requires that you are alert all the way as you can easily burn your food in these.
If you don't have any cast iron pots or pans, buy them second handed if you can as they get better as they age. The pots and pans I use are the same ones my great-grandmother used to cook with, so you take good care of them, they'll last for a long time.

When you're done cooking with them, let them cool down before you wash them, do not, I repeat, do not rinse a hot cast iron pot or pan in cold water while it's still hot. It can explode! Let it cool down some and then you can rinse it in lukewarm but preferably hot water. Also, avoid using soap (Washing up liquid?), it will make the iron brittle. However, if you cooked fish in your pans and want to get rid of the smell, use only a tiny amount of soap and when you have dried it with paper towels (cloth towels will be ruined and letting it dry on its own is as sure way to get rust.), take paper towels, add some vegetable oil (or olive, up to you) and rub it onto the pot or pan.

When it comes to the non-stick pans, I'm a little more sceptical, but if you're going to use it, use either wooden tools or plastic with soft edges, just to be on safe side.

Bread & "Sandwich cake"

Skagencake (SE: Skagentårta)

This delicious cake can be served as an entry or main course. The name Skagen is from an area in Denmark, that's strongly associated with seafood. You can of course make a lot of variants of this cake, but this is my personal favourite.

Ingredients

Base

200 grams of dark rye bread (SE:Kavring)

75 grams of melted butter

Filling

200 grams of cream cheese

250 grams of cottage cheese

3 tablespoons of freshly grated horseradish

300 grams of freshly peeled shrimps

150 grams chopped Crayfish tails

½ dl of finely chopped dill

½ Teaspoon of salt

1 ml pepper

Decoration

50 grams of lumpfish roe

Some whole dill

Some shrimps or Crayfish tails

How to do

1. Crumble the rye bread into a bowl or a Food processor.
2. Melt the butter and mix with the bread to a dough.
3. Put the dough in a round baking tin or baking sheet, depending on what shape you want your cake to have, just make sure it's spread evenly. Let it rest somewhere cold for about an hour.

4. Mix the ingredients that goes into the filling, stir carefully so the ingredients are spread around more.
5. Use a palette or knife to smear the filling across the dough, make sure it's even and smooth. Let it rest in the fridge for a couple of hours or, preferably, overnight.
6. Garnish with the Dill, Shrimps or Crayfish tails

Hint

Drop some lemon juice onto the shrimps before mixing them with the other ingredients.

Ham, cheese and grapes are a common garnish in Sweden and works well with this cake as well.

Skattkärrslimpa

Now, this bread I tried to translate, but apparently there isn't an English equivalent to the Swedish name. It's a loaf of bread, that much I can translate.

Ingredients

1 L of water

½ dl oil

1 dl syrup

100 grams of yeast

1 tablespoon of salt

1 kg flour

6 hg of sifted rye

How to do

Heat the water to 37° Celsius, mix syrup and oil into the water.

Pour the liquid into a bowl and mix in the yeast.

Add salt, flour and mix.

Pour the sifted rye and mix well.

Pour some flour onto a baking table (or any clean flat surface) Put the dough on the surface and work it with your hands. (takes between 15 to 30 minutes to knead it well)

Cut the dough in 4 pieces and form every piece to a loaf.

Put the 4 loafs on a baking sheet with some baking paper beneath

Put them in a COLD OVEN!! (Important!)

Set the oven to 200° Celsius when you have placed the loafs in the oven.

Let them bake in the oven for about 40 to 45 minutes

Crispbread

This recipe is marvellous if you want to be somewhat healthy and still enjoy your sandwich

Ingredients

2 dl oats

2 dl rye flour

3½ dl oat bran

2 dl flaxseed

2½ dl sesame seeds

2½ dl sunflower seeds

2½ dl Pumpkin seeds

2 teaspoons of salt

7 dl water

How to do

Heat the oven to 150° Celsius

All the ingredients are mixed together in a bowl

Spread the dough evenly on a baking paper that's on a baking tray.

Put the tray in the oven for an hour

Take it out and let it rest a little

Sour milk bread

I know, doesn't sound appetizing. But sour milk is popular to have for breakfast in Sweden, and this bread is so delicious.

Ingredients

1 L of sour milk

1½ teaspoon of bicarbonate

2 dl of dark syrup

2 teaspoons of salt

7 dl strong flour

3 dl graham flour

3 dl course rye flour

1 dl sunflower seeds

1 dl crushed rye

1 dl flaxseed

1 dl hazelnuts (Can be switched for more sunflower seeds)

1½ dl Raisin

How to do

Heat the oven to 175° Celsius

Mix sour milk, bicarbonate and syrup in a bowl

Mix all the other ingredients in a separate bowl

Mix the two bowls together

Grease two bread molds with butter and coat with flour

Pour the dough into each of the molds

Put in the oven for 1½ to 2 hours

Use a kitchen needle to check if it's done. If no liquid on the needle, it's done.

Hint

After about half the time have passed you can cover the bread with some baking sheet.

Main courses

Beef with mashed potatoes with västerbottenost (Swedish delicacy cheese)

Ingredients

Mashed potatoes

2L water

½ tablespoon of salt

1 kg peeled "Almond" potato or any floury potatoes (King Edward for instance)

1 chopped leek

2 dl heavy cream

1 dl chopped parsley leaf

50g grated Västerbotten cheese (or an equally flavour rich cheese)

2 teaspoons of sea salt

2 ml freshly grounded black pepper

Beef

4 pieces beef around 200g each

2ml of salt

2ml of freshly grounded black pepper

2 tablespoons of freshly chopped thyme

1 tablespoon of olive oil

How to do

Mashed potatoes

Put the potatoes in a saucepan, fill with water and add salt bring to a boil, add leek then boil for about 15 minutes.

Pour the potatoes and leeks in a colander, let it rest and steam off for about 5 minutes before you put them back in the saucepan.

Add the cream, butter, parsley leaf, and the cheese in the saucepan and mix by whisking with an eggbeater.

Add salt and pepper after your preferred taste.

Beef

Bring out the beef from the fridge let it thaw in room temperature for about 1 hour.

Salt and pepper and sprinkle thyme on each side of the beef

Drizzle the olive oil over the meat and make sure that oil and spices are evenly applied.

Heat a frying pan on high heat until it nearly smokes from it. Add the meat and after frying the meat 1 minute on each side, lower the heat to medium.

Fry the meat then 2 to 3 minutes on each side, pending on how you prefer your meat. Put the beef in tin foil and let them rest for 10 minutes before serving.

Goulash soup

A delicious soup that I enjoy during winter time.

Ingredients

200g of beef

1 tablespoon of oil

Salt & Pepper

1 yellow onion

1 red bell pepper

½ to 2 garlic clove(s)

0.25 teaspoons of cumin

1.5 tablespoons of tomato puree

Cayenne pepper

0.5 l water

1 stock cube of beef stock

2 potatoes

2 slices of rye bread

How to do

1. Make sure to remove any remaining tendons from the beef and cut it in small cubes. Finely chop the onion and the bell pepper.
2. Fry the meat in some cooking oil in a pot, add salt and pepper. Add onion and bell pepper after a while. Use a mortar to crush the garlic with the cumin, then add the tomato puree and cayenne pepper.
3. Put the garlic and tomato mix into the pot with the meat and put aside for now.
4. Put the water to boil and add the stock cube in the hot water. Pour half of the stock over the meat and let it boil under lid for 20 minutes.
5. Peel and chop the potatoes coarsely. Add the potatoes and the remaining of the stock to the meat and boil under lid for 30 minutes.
6. Serve the soup with some bread.

Potato pancake with pork

Done properly, it can be one of the most delicious dishes you can have.

Ingredients

800g of non-floury potatoes (Asterix is a good example)

2dl of flour

1 teaspoon of salt

4 dl whole milk

1 egg

600g of salted pork bellies

Butter for cooking

Lingonberries

5 dl Lingonberries

2 dl of sugar

How to do

1. Peel the potato
2. Whisk flour, salt and some of the milk together into a smooth batter. Then add the rest of milk and the egg.
3. Fry the pork in a frying pan and keep it warm. Save the grease to the frying of the pancakes.
4. Grate the potato coarsely into the egg-batter.
5. Fry some butter along with the pork grease and add small amounts of the batter to the pan. Around ½ dl batter per cake.
6. Even the cakes using a Spatula and fry them on medium heat until golden on each side.

Lingonberries

1. Add the lingonberries and sugar and stir until the berries are mushy and the sugar dissolved. Will stay fresh in the fridge for weeks.

Serve the pancakes with the pork and the berries.

Mexican wrap

Delicious and custom to have on Friday evenings in Sweden

Ingredients

1 finely chopped yellow onion

300g minced beef

2 diced bell peppers

1 can of mashed tomatoes

1 tablespoon of tomato puree

100g grated cheese

1 stock cube

1 teaspoon of oregano

1 tablespoon of Japanese soy

1 garlic clove

10 drops of tabasco

Misc ingredients

4 Tortillas

Canned corn

Finely chopped and rinsed salad

Sliced tomatoes

Jalapeños

How to do

Fry the onion and the meat on medium heat. Add salt and pepper, add the stock cube.

Add the mashed tomatoes, bell pepper, soy sauce, tomato puree, crushed garlic and the tabasco.

Boil intensely with no lid for 5 to 10 minutes, add a little water in case it becomes to dry.

Put some salad, corn, tomato and if you like, jalapeños on a tortilla bread.

Add the meat to the tortilla and some grated cheese.

Savoury chicken pie

A very good pie both warm and cold.

Ingredients

Pie crust

3 dl of flour

125g of butter

2 to 3 tablespoons of water

Filling

Pre-cooked whole chicken

½ large leek

1 red bell pepper

1 can of mushrooms (SE: Champinjoner)

2 tablespoons of butter

2 tablespoons of flour

2 & ½ dl cooking cream + the juice from the mushroom

Salt

Pepper

Powdered bell pepper

How to do

Mix the ingredients to the crust in a bowl, let it rest in the fridge for 30 minutes. Carve the chicken into smaller pieces. Shred the bell pepper and the leek. Separate the mushroom from its broth, save the broth.

Fry mushroom, leek and bell pepper in butter. Sprinkle the flour and stir thoroughly, otherwise the flour can make lumps. Dilute with cream and mushroom broth. Add salt, pepper and powdered bell pepper after your liking. Boil for 5 minutes.

Heat the oven to 200º Celsius. Put the pie dough evenly in a pie tin, and use a fork to prick holes in the bottom of the dough. Pre-bake the crust for about 10 minutes.

Now, mix the chicken meat into the stew, then add the mix into the crust and return it to the oven and bake it for 20 minutes.

Green pepper chicken

Lovely dish with a little spicy touch.

Ingredients

1 whole grilled chicken or 3 oven baked chicken fillets

Sauce

2 Tablespoons of dried green pepper

1 Tablespoon of Dijon mustard

2 dl of cream

3 Tablespoons of Chinese soy sauce

1 Teaspoon of cayenne pepper

How to do

Grind the pepper in a mortar.

Mix all the ingredients for the sauce in a sauce pan and bring to a boil and let it boil for 5 minutes.

Shred or dice the chicken and add to the sauce. Let it simmer for 5 minutes.

Serve with rice and a nice salad.

Smoked pork stew with rice

This form of smoked pork is referred to as Kassler in Swedish or Kasseler in German. Either way, it's delicious.

Ingredients

500g of Smoked pork/ Kassler

1 Clove of garlic

2 Teaspoons of curry

1 dl water

1 Vegetable stock cube

1 to 2 Tablespoons of tomato puree

2 & ½ dl of cooking cream

2 & ½ dl of crème fraiche

1 red bell pepper

Pepper

Soy sauce

How to do

Shred the pork and fry it with the garlic and curry in a pot.

Add the vegetable stock and water.

Then add the tomato puree, cream and crème fraiche, bring it to a boil and let it boil for 5 minutes.

Shred the bell pepper and add to the stew.

Add pepper and soy sauce after your own liking.

Serve with rice.

Black currant stew

From what I've learned, black and red currant aren't common in the USA, so I apologize for any American readers, but I hope you can get the currants imported. It's worth it.

Ingredients

500g of pork loin

150g of celeriac

3 carrots

2 Tablespoons of soy sauce

1 dl of undiluted black currant juice

2 dl of water

1 beef stock cube

1 ml of pepper

1 bay leaf

½ Teaspoon of thyme

1 dl of chopped leek

1 Tablespoon of potato flour

How to do

Pour the soy sauce, juice and water in a pot.

Add the stock cube and the spices, bring it to a boil.

Shred the meat and dice the root crops.

Cut the leek.

Add the meat and root crop in the simmering liquid and let it simmer for 10 minutes.

Add the leek and simmer for another 5 minutes.

Mix the potato flour with some water and stir it into the pot.

Bring it up to a quick boil so the sauce thickens.

Serve with potatoes.

Vegetarian stew from Morocco

I'm normally not one to enjoy vegetarian dishes, but this one really hit the right spot for my taste.

Ingredients

300g of quorn mince

1 small eggplant/aubergine

1 yellow onion

1 can of mashed tomatoes

2 cloves of garlic

2 Teaspoons of cumin

2 Teaspoons of powdered bell pepper

3 Teaspoons of curry

Salt and pepper

How to do

Start with cutting the eggplant into small dices, but it in a bowl and sprinkle some salt over it and let it rest for a while, this will remove part of the liquid in the eggplant.

Chop the yellow onion and fry it in pot with some oil, until it's soft. Then add the eggplant and let it cook for a few minutes. Then add the quorn and some salt and pepper. Just remember that you already had salt on the eggplant so go easy on the salt.

Mash the garlic into the pot, then add the mashed tomatoes followed by cumin, powdered bell pepper and curry.

If you like spicy food, now is the time to add the spices you like, otherwise, skip to the next step.

Let it simmer on low heat under lid for 15 minutes.

Serve with couscous and salad.

Dessert and cakes

I generally have a weak interest in desserts, but there are some desserts that I just love, be it pies or puddings.

Lemon & Lime pie

A refreshing dessert, perfect for summertime

Ingredients

Crust

3 dl of flour

2 Tablespoons of unrefined sugar

125g of room temperate butter (soft butter)

1 egg yolk

Stuffing

3 eggs

2 dl unrefined sugar

2 Teaspoons of vanilla sugar

2 dl heavy cream

1 lime

1 lemon

Garnish

1 lime

Icing sugar

Whipped cream

How to do

1. Make the pie crust. Mix the sugar, butter and flour to a grainy dough, add the egg yolk and work it into a dough.
2. Put the dough in a pie tin and put it in the fridge for 30 minutes or the freezer for 10 minutes
3. Meanwhile, whisk eggs and sugar to a fluffy batter, stir flour, vanilla sugar and the cream into the batter.
4. Heat the oven to 200° Celsius. Grate the peelings of both the lime and lemon and squeeze out the juices of both. Add that to the batter and whisk it evenly. Pour it into the pie crust.
5. Bake it on the lower part of the oven for 30 minutes. Take it out and let it cool. Garnish the pie by sifting icing sugar over it and put some sliced lime on it.

Serve the pie lukewarm or cold with whipped cream.

Bread pudding

Classical dessert during autumn and winter in Sweden.

Ingredients

10 slices of slightly stale white bread.

1, 25 dl cream

8,75 dl of whole milk

1,25 dl sugar

5 eggs

3, 75 dl raisin, chopped dry apricots and prunes

10 squares of dark chocolate (70% cacao)

2,5 ml cinnamon or vanilla

How to do

1. Heat the oven to 175° Celsius. Cut the bread in cubes. Chop the apricots and prunes and soak them in some rum if you prefer, otherwise milk.
2. Whisk cream, milk, sugar and egg together. Flavour with vanilla or cinnamon. Evenly distribute the bread cubes in an ovenproof bowl along with the bits of fruit.
3. Pour the egg mixture over the bread and fruit. Top it with coarsely chopped chocolate. Bake in the oven for 20 minutes or until the egg mixture has solidified some and the pudding turned fluffy. Take it out and let it cool.

Serve with some vanilla ice cream.

Gooseberry pie

A very delicious pie to have with some whipped cream or vanilla ice cream during summer.

Ingredients

Crust

6 dl of flour

1 ml of salt

75 grams of butter

75 grams of lard

1 tablespoon of sugar

1 egg yolk

Cold water

Stuffing

1 ½ litres or 750 grams of gooseberry

1½ dl sugar

Grated peel of lemon

A few drops of bitter almond essence or 1-2 grated bitter almonds (Use essence if you're allergic or don't use it at all as I don't think it affects the flavour that much)

Icing

1 tablespoon of milk

1 table spoon of sugar

How to do

Heat the oven to 225° C

Crust

Mix flour and salt in a bowl, add butter and lard and work it together with your fingertips to a grainy substance. Add sugar, egg yolk and some water if needed to stabilize the mix to a soft dough.

Shape the dough to a ball shape, sprinkle some flour on it and wrap it in saran wrap and let it rest in the fridge for at least an hour.

After at least an hour has passed, take the dough out and cut it in three pieces. Roll some of it on a lightly floured table and put the flattened dough in a rather high edged pie tray that can hold at least a litre. Save the rest of the dough for later.

Stuffing

Clean the gooseberries, mix them in a bowl with sugar, grated lemon peel and bitter almond (if you choose to have it in) and add half of the mixture in the pie tray. Now roll another set of dough and place it on top of the mixture, then add the last of the berries.

Now roll the last piece of dough and place it on top of the mix, brush the edge with some water and make sure it's tight. Make a hole in the middle of the pie so the air can escape while baking. Brush the top of it with some milk and sprinkle sugar on the top.

Baking

Bake the pie 15 minutes in 225° C, then lower the heat to 175° C and bake for another 30 minutes or until the crust is golden brown. Use a fork or knife to check if the pie is ready, the berries should feel soft when it's ready. Take it out and let it cool for 10 minutes, serve it with custard, cream or ice cream.

Afterword

Well, this has been fun. I really loved writing this book and I hope you enjoyed reading it as well as testing the recipes that I have collected in this little book.

I'd like to thank my mother, Martina Rosendahl for her many advices while writing this book.

The teachers and counsellors at SVF for helping me learn to live independent (they focus on persons with autism) https://www.svf.fhsk.se/

My brothers who I've been nagging on while writing this book.

I hope to see you again soon dear reader.

Regards

Viktor Schönberg

"The autist's cookbook, recipes and tips for those in the autism spectrum"

Second edition

Copyright © 2017 by Viktor Schönberg
All rights reserved. This book or any portion thereof
may not be reproduced or used in any manner whatsoever
without the express written permission of the publisher
except for the use of brief quotations in a book review.

Printed in Great Britain
by Amazon